Beaded Strings, *page 22*

Table of Contents

2 Festive Mat

4 Cool Water Mat

6 Happy-Go-Lucky Mat

8 Mouse Mat

10 Colorful Muff

12 Fidget Cuff

13 Tags & Bobbles Cuff

15 Bowl of Cherries Muff

Embellishments

16 Sunburst

17 Hearts

18 Curlicue

18 Zinnia

19 Pompoms

19 Tassel

20 Fish

21 Frilly Flower

22 Beaded Strings

22 Star

23 Covered Rings

24 Mouse

25 Floral Delight

26 Cherries

General Information

27 Stitch Guide

28 Metric Conversion Charts

A Note From the Editors

The number of Americans living with Alzheimer's disease is growing. It is estimated that 5.5 million Americans of all ages have Alzheimer's disease. In the United States alone, there are nearly 15 million Alzheimer's and dementia caregivers. Both Judy and I have been caretakers for a parent with Alzheimer's and felt strongly that we wanted to create a book that might possibly help in some small way.

Every person with Alzheimer's disease experiences the disease differently. Since Alzheimer's affects people in different ways, the stages don't always fall into neat boxes and the symptoms might vary—each person will progress through the stages differently.

The most common system, developed by Dr. Barry Reisberg of New York University, breaks the progression of Alzheimer's disease into seven stages. For more information on these stages, check out www.alzheimers.net/stages-of-alzheimers-disease.

Agitation often develops in the middle stages of Alzheimer's. Some patients respond to music and pet therapy. The original Twiddle® Muff was developed by Margaret Light for her grandmother, Lily, and satisfied her need to keep her hands warm and busy.

It is our hope that the muffs, mats and cuffs found in *Fiddle Mats, Muffs & Cuffs* will calm the agitation and anxiety Alzheimer's patients suffer from and give them something to do with their hands to keep them busy.

These projects are perfect for using up your scrap yarns. Please contact your local nursing home or Alzheimer's care units to donate and make a difference.

Connie Ellis
Judy Crow,

D1214667

Festive Mat, *page 2*

Festive Mat

Design by Annie's

Skill Level

 **EASY**

Finished Measurements

11½ inches wide x 17 inches long

Materials

- Hobby Lobby I Love this Yarn! medium (worsted) weight acrylic yarn (7 oz/355 yds/198g per skein):
    1 skein #788 limelight
- Size J/10/6mm crochet hook
- Tapestry needle
- Materials needed for each Embellishment used

Gauge

Gauge is not important for this project.

Pattern Notes

Use 2 strands of yarn held together throughout for Mat only.

Chain-2 at end of row counts as first double crochet unless otherwise stated.

Embellish as desired or as shown using listed Embellishments.

Embellishments Used

1 Sunburst *(on page 16)*

1 Large Heart with Curlicue in center *(on pages 17 and 18)*

1 Zinnia with bead in center *(on page 18)*

1 Beaded String with flower button *(on page 22)*

3 large Pompoms *(on page 19)*

4 Tassels *(on page 19)*

Mat

Row 1 (RS): Holding 2 strands tog *(see Pattern Notes)* ch 30, working in **back bar of ch** *(see illustration)*, dc in 3rd ch from hook *(2 sk chs count as a dc)* and in each rem ch. Turn. *(29 dc)*

Back Bar of Chain

Row 2: Sl st in first dc, dc in next dc; *sl st in next dc, dc in next dc; rep from * to beg 2 sk chs; sl st in 2nd ch of beg 2 sk chs. **Ch 2** *(see Pattern Notes)*, turn.

Row 3: Dc in each dc and in each sl st, turn.

Row 4: Sl st in first dc, dc in next dc; *sl st in next dc, dc in next dc; rep from * to turning ch-2; sl st in 2nd ch of turning ch-2. Ch 2, turn.

Row 5: Dc in each dc and in each sl st, turn.

Rep rows 4 and 5 until piece measures 17 inches long. At end of last row, do not ch 2, do not turn. Fasten off.

Embellish as desired or as shown in photo. ●

Cool Water Mat

Design by Annie's

Skill Level

Finished Measurements

12 inches wide x 17 inches long

Materials

- Medium (worsted) weight acrylic yarn:
  2½ oz/130 yds/70g each orange and turquoise
- Size J/10/6mm crochet hook or size needed to obtain gauge
- 4 jingle bells
- 30 inches ¼-inch-wide ribbon of your choice
- Tapestry needle
- Materials listed with each Embellishment used

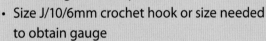

Gauge

11 dc = 4 inches; 5 dc rows = 3 inches

Pattern Notes

Use 2 strands of yarn held together throughout for Mat.

Join with slip stitch as indicated unless otherwise stated.

Chain-4 at beginning of row counts as first treble crochet unless otherwise stated.

Chain-3 at beginning of row counts as first double crochet unless otherwise stated.

Embellish as desired or as shown using listed Embellishments.

Special Stitch

Cross stitch (cross st): Sk next st, tr in next st, ch 1, working behind tr just made, work tr in sk st.

Embellishments Used

1 Fish (*on page 20*)

1 large Pompom (*on page 19*)

1 Frilly Flower with braided tails (*on page 21*)

1 Beaded String (*on page 22*)

2 Small Hearts (*on page 17*)

Mat

Row 1: With **2 strands orange held tog** (*see Pattern Notes*), ch 48, dc in 3rd ch from hook (*first 2 chs do not count as dc*), dc in each ch across, turn. Fasten off. (*46 dc*)

Row 2: Join (*see Pattern Notes*) turquoise in first st, **ch 4** (*see Pattern Notes*), **cross st** (*see Special Stitch*) across to last dc, tr in last dc, turn (*2 tr, 22 cross sts*)

Row 3: Ch 1, sc in first 2 tr, *sk next ch, sc in next 2 tr, rep from * across, ending last sc in 4th ch of ch-4, turn.

Row 4: Ch 3 (*see Pattern Notes*), dc in each st across, turn. (*46 dc*)

Rows 5–8: Rep row 4.

Row 9: Ch 4, cross st across, ending with tr in 4th ch of beg ch-4, turn. (*2 tr, 22 cross sts*)

Row 10: Ch 1, sc in first 2 sts, *sk next ch-1, sc in next 2 tr, rep from * across, sc in last st, turn.

Rows 11–16: Ch 3, dc in each sc across, ending with a dc in the last sc, turn.

Row 17: Rep row 9.

Row 18: Rep row 10. Fasten off. *(46 sc)*

Row 19: Join orange, ch 3, dc in each sc across, fasten off. *(46 dc)*

Finishing

Cut ribbon into 6 lengths each 5 inches long. Fold each length in half to form lp.

Tack ends of 3 lps to each short edge of Mat as shown in photo.

Tack 1 bell to each corner.

Embellish as desired or as shown in photo. ●

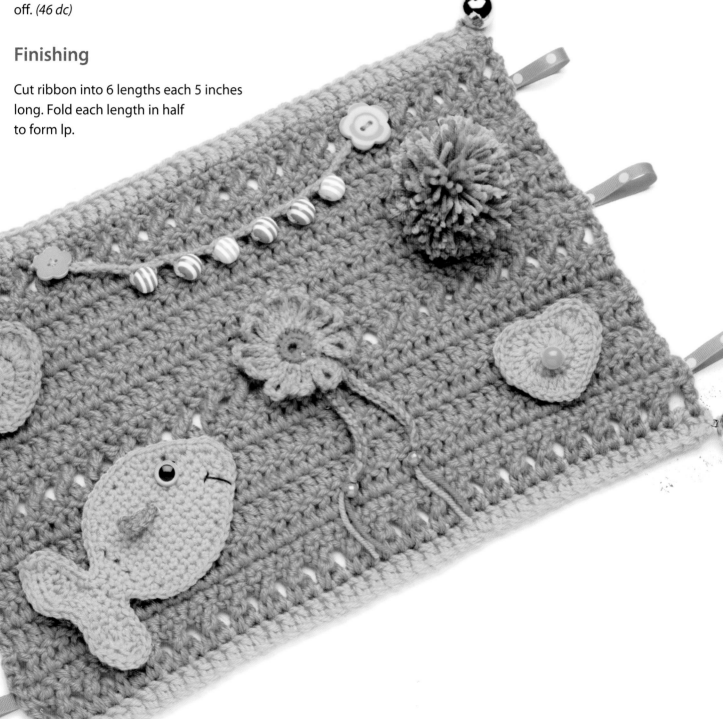

Happy-Go-Lucky Mat

Design by Annie's

Skill Level

 ⬛⬛⬜⬜ EASY

Finished Measurements

16½ inches wide x 14 inches long

Materials

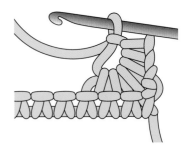

- Medium (worsted) weight acrylic yarn:
    10 oz/520 yds/280g multicolored
- Size J/10/6mm crochet hook or size needed to obtain gauge
- 3½ yds ¼-inch-wide ribbon of your choice
- Tapestry needle
- Materials listed for each Embellishment used

Gauge

7 star sts = 4 inches; 4 rows in pattern = 4 inches

Pattern Notes

Double crochet at end of odd-numbered rows is worked in same stitch as last step of star base.

Chain-2 at beginning of each even-numbered row does not count as a stitch.

Join with slip stitch as indicated unless otherwise stated.

Hold 2 strands together throughout pattern for Mat.

Embellish as desired or as shown using listed Embellishments.

Special Stitches

Beginning star stitch (beg star st): Insert hook in 2nd ch from hook, pull up lp, [insert hook in next ch and pull up lp] 4 times, yo and draw through all 6 lps on hook, ch 1 to secure.

Star stitch (star st): Insert hook in ch-1 of last star st, pull up lp, insert hook in side of last lp of last star st and pull up lp, insert hook in st at base of last lp of last star st and pull up lp, [insert hook in next st and pull up lp] twice, yo, draw through all 6 lps on hook, ch 1 to secure.

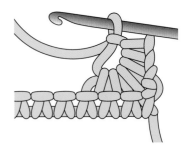

Beginning Star Stitch

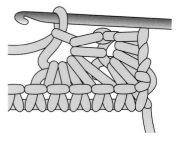

Star Stitch

Embellishments Used

4 medium Pompoms *(on page 19)*

1 Zinnia *(on page 18)*

1 Star with bead in center *(on page 22)*

1 Small Heart with bead in center *(on page 17)*

1 Covered Ring with braided tails *(on page 23)*

1 flower button with bead tails *(on page 22)*

Mat

Row 1: Holding 2 strands tog *(see Pattern Notes)* ch 50, **beg star st** *(see Special Stitches)* in 2nd ch from hook and in next 4 chs, ***star st** *(see Special Stitches)* in previous star st and in next 2 chs, rep from * across, **dc in last ch** *(see Pattern Notes)* at base of last lp of last star st, turn. *(23 star sts)*

Row 2: Ch 2 *(see Pattern Notes)*, *2 hdc in ch-1 of next star st, rep from * across to beg ch-2, hdc in 2nd ch of beg ch-2, turn.

Row 3: Ch 3, beg star st in 2nd and 3rd chs from hook and in first 3 sts, *star st in previous star st and in next 2 sts, rep from * across, dc in last hdc at base of last lp of last star st, turn.

Rows 4–25: [Rep rows 2 and 3] alternately.

Row 26: Rep row 2. At end of last row, do not turn.

Edging

Rnd 1 (RS): Evenly sc around entire Mat, working 3 sc in each corner, **join** *(see Pattern Notes)* in first st.

Rnd 2: Ch 1, **reverse sc** *(see Stitch Guide)* in each st around, join in first st. Fasten off.

Finishing

Cut 22 pieces of ribbon each 5 inches in length. Fold each length in half to form lp and tack ends to back of Mat.

Tack 4 lps to each short edge and 5 lps to each long edge with 1 lp in each corner of Mat.

Tack Embellishments to Mat as desired or as shown in photo. ●

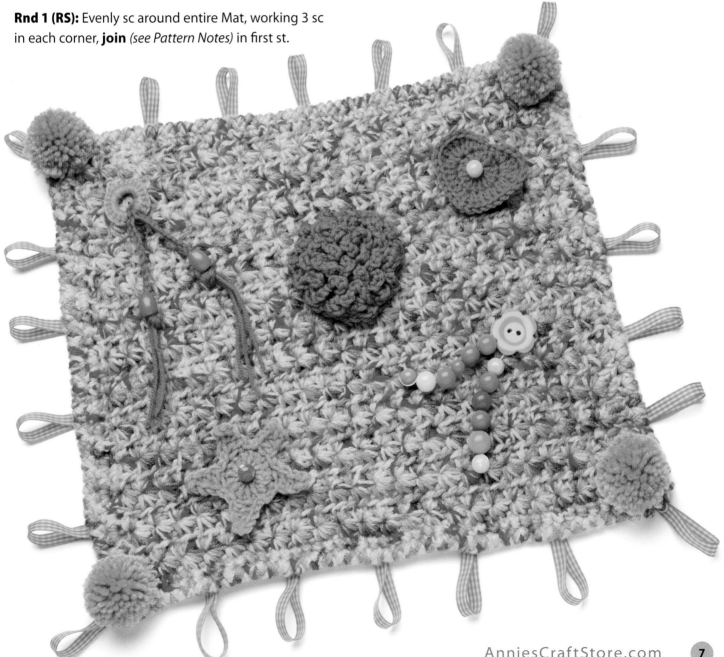

Mouse Mat

Design by Annie's

Skill Level

 EASY

Finished Measurements

16 inches wide x 13 inches long

Materials

- Hobby Lobby I Love This Yarn! medium (worsted) weight acrylic yarn (5 oz/252 yds/142g per skein):
    2 skeins #953 fuchsia neon
- Size J/10/6mm crochet hook or size needed to obtain gauge
- 2 yds ¼-inch-wide ribbon of choice
- Tapestry needle
- Materials listed with each Embellishment used

Gauge

6 sts in pattern = 2 inches; 6 pattern rows = 6 inches

Pattern Notes

Hold 2 strands together throughout for Mat.

Embellish as desired or as shown using listed Embellishments.

Special Stitches

First foundation half double crochet (first foundation hdc): Ch 2, yo, insert hook into 2nd ch from hook *(see illustration A)*, yo, pull up lp, yo, pull through 1 lp on hook *(see illustration B—ch-1 completed)*, yo, pull through all lps on hook *(see illustrations C and D—hdc completed)*.

Next foundation half double crochet (next foundation hdc): *Yo, insert hook in last ch-1 made *(see illustration A)*, yo, pull up lp, yo, pull through 1 lp on hook *(see illustration B—ch-1 completed)*, yo, pull through all lps on hook *(see illustrations C and D—hdc completed)*, rep from * as indicated.

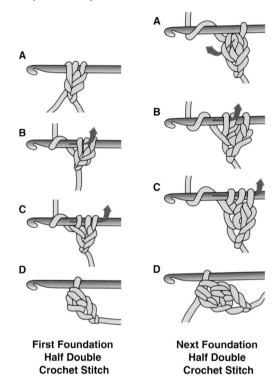

First Foundation Half Double Crochet Stitch

Next Foundation Half Double Crochet Stitch

Embellishments Used

2 large Pompoms with beaded tails *(on page 19)*

10 Covered Rings *(on page 23)*

1 Mouse *(on page 24)*

1 Large Heart *(on page 17)*

Mat

Row 1: Holding 2 strands tog *(see Pattern Notes)*, work **first foundation hdc** *(see Special Stitches)*, work **next foundation hdc** *(see Special Stitches)* 47 times, turn. *(48 hdc)*

Row 2 (RS): Ch 1, hdc in first st, *hdc in **front lp** *(see Stitch Guide)* of each of next 2 sts**, hdc in **back lp** *(see Stitch Guide)* of each of next 2 sts, rep from * across, ending last rep at **, hdc in both lps of last st, turn.

Row 3: Ch 1, hdc in both lps of first st, *hdc in back lp of each of next 2 sts**, hdc in front lp of each of next 2 sts, rep from * across, ending last rep at **, hdc in both lps of last st, turn.

Next rows: Rep rows 2 and 3 alternately until piece measures 13 inches from beg, ending with row 2. At end of last row, do not turn. Fasten off.

Cut ribbon in 4 pieces each 18 inches long. Tie ribbon into 4 bows, tack 1 in each corner.

Tack Embellishments to Mat as desired or as shown in photo. ●

Colorful Muff

Design by Annie's

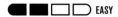
Finished Measurements

8 inches long x 12 inches in circumference

Materials

- Medium (worsted) weight acrylic yarn:
  3 oz/160 yds/85g each turquoise, pink, orange, lime and multicolored
- Size J/10/6mm crochet hook
- 22 inches of ¼-inch-wide ribbon of choice (optional)
- Tapestry needle
- Stitch markers

Gauge

Gauge is not important for this project.

Pattern Notes

Hold 2 strands of yarn together throughout for Cuff.

Weave in ends as work progresses.

Chain-3 at beginning of round or row counts as first double crochet unless otherwise stated.

Join with slip stitch as indicated unless otherwise stated.

Draw up yarn on fans to current round.

Work into top of each fan and not into skipped stitch behind fan.

Special Stitches

Bobble: Yo, insert hook in indicated st and draw up lp, yo, pull through 2 lps, [yo, insert hook in same st and draw up a lp, yo and draw through 2 lps] 4 times, yo and pull through 6 lps on hook, ch 1 *(does not count as a st)* to close.

Fan: Insert hook in st 1 rnd below and 2 sts to right of current st, yo and **draw up a lp** *(see Pattern Notes)*, insert hook in st 2 rnds below and 1 st to right of current st, yo and draw up a lp, insert hook in st 3 rnds below current st, yo and draw up a lp, insert hook in st 2 rnds below and 1 st to right of current st, yo and draw up a lp, insert hook in st 1 rnd below and 2 sts to left of current st, yo and draw up a lp, yo, pull through all lps on hook.

Muff

Ribbing

Row 1 (RS): Holding 2 strands tog *(see Pattern Notes)* with turquoise, ch 5, working in **back lps** *(see Stitch Guide)*, sc in 2nd ch from hook and in each ch across, turn. *(4 sc)*

Row 2: Ch 1, working in back lps, sc in each sc across, turn.

Rep row 2 until piece measures 10 inches or desired circumference.

Joining row: Ch 1, with RS tog and working through opposite side of foundation ch and back lp of last row, sl st in each st across, turn. Turn piece RS out.

Arm

Rnd 1: Now working in rnds and working in ends of rows, ch 1, 32 sc evenly sp around, **join** *(see Pattern Notes)* in beg sc *(31 sc)* Place marker on first st and move up as each rnd is completed.

Rnds 2 & 3: Hdc in first st, sc in each rem st around, do not join.

Rnd 4: Hdc in first st, sc in each rem st around, join in beg hdc. Fasten off.

Rnd 5: Join *(2 strands held tog)* pink in last st, hdc in first st, **fpdc** *(see Stitch Guide)* in next st 2 rnds below, *sc in next st, fpdc in next st 2 rnds below, rep from * around, do not join. *(16 fpdc)*

Rnd 6: Rep rnd 2. *(1 hdc, 31 sc)*

Rnd 7: Working in back lps, hdc in first st, sc in each rem st around, join in beg hdc. Fasten off.

Rnd 8: Join multicolored in last st, **ch 3** *(see Pattern Notes)*, dc in each st around, join in top of ch-3. *(32 dc)*

Rnd 9: Sc in each st around, do not join. *(32 sc)*

Rnd 10: Hdc in first st, sc in each of next 3 sts, ***bobble** *(see Special Stitches)* in next st, sc in each of next 3 sts, rep from * around to last 3 sts, sc in next 2 sts, bobble in last st. Fasten off.

Rnd 11: Join orange in last st, rep rnd 2. *(1 hdc, 31 sc)*

Rnd 12: Working in back lps, hdc in first st, sc in each rem st around. *(1 hdc, 31 sc)*

Rnds 13–15: Rep rnd 2.

Rnd 16: Rep rnd 4.

Rnd 17: Join lime in last st, hdc in first st, sc in next st, ***fan** *(see Special Stitches)*, sk next st *(behind fan)*, sc in each of next 4 sts, rep from * around to last 3 sts, fan in next st, sc in each of last 2 sts. *(6 fans)*

Rnds 18 & 19: Rep rnd 2. Fasten off in last st.

Finishing

Fold piece RS tog, working through both sides, sl st in each st across. Fasten off.

Thread ribbon through sts on last row of turquoise ribbing. ●

Gauge

Gauge is not important for this project.

Pattern Notes

Work in multiple of 2 plus 1

Hold 2 strands of yarn together throughout.

Weave in ends as work progresses.

Chain-3 at beginning of row counts as first double crochet unless otherwise stated.

Embellish as desired or as shown using listed Embellishments.

Special Stitch

V-stitch (V-st): (Dc, ch 1, dc) in same st.

Embellishments Used

1 each small, medium and large Pompom *(on page 19)*

1 Curlicue *(on page 18)*

1 Frilly Flower *(on page 21)*

1 dragonfly button

Cuff

Row 1 (RS): Holding 2 strands tog *(see Pattern Notes)* ch 25, sc in 2nd ch from hook and in each ch across, **ch 3** *(see Pattern Notes)*, turn. *(24 sc)*

Row 2: V-st *(see Special Stitch)* in next sc, *sk next sc, V-st in next st, rep from * across, ch 3, turn

Row 3: *V-st in ch-1 sp of each V-st across, dc in last st, ch 3, turn

Rep row 3 until piece is 9 inches long or desired length. Leaving long end, fasten off.

Finishing

Fold piece in half, RS tog, using tapestry needle and long end, sew Cuff tog down entire length. Turn RS out. Embellish as desired or as shown in photo using Embellishments listed. ●

Fidget Cuff

Design by Annie's

Skill Level

 EASY

Finished Measurements

9 inches long x 11 inches in circumference

Materials

- Medium (worsted) weight acrylic yarn:
    3 oz/160 yds/85g orange
- Size K/10½/6.5mm crochet hook
- Tapestry needle
- Stitch markers
- Materials listed for each Embellishment used

4 MEDIUM

Tags & Bobbles Cuff

Design by Annie's

Skill Level

 ◼◼◻◻ EASY

Finished Measurements

9 inches long x 12 inches in circumference

Materials

- Medium (worsted) weight acrylic yarn:
    5 oz/200g color of choice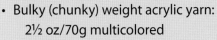
- Bulky (chunky) weight acrylic yarn:
    2½ oz/70g multicolored
- Sizes F/5/3.75mm and J/10/6mm crochet hooks
- 1 yard of ½-inch-wide ribbon of choice
- 24 large-hole assorted oval beads
- Tapestry needle
- Stitch markers

Gauge

Gauge is not important for this project.

Pattern Notes

Hold 2 strands of worsted yarn together throughout.

Use 1 strand chunky yarn throughout.

Weave in ends as work progresses.

Chain-2 at beginning of row counts as first double crochet unless otherwise stated.

Join with slip stitch as indicated unless otherwise stated.

Special Stitches

Cluster (cl): Holding back last lp of each st on hook, 4 dc as indicated, yo, draw through all 5 lps on hook. Push cl to RS.

Bead single crochet (bead sc): Change to F hook, insert hook through bead, moving bead up the shaft of the hook, insert hook into indicated st, yo, pull up lp, yo, pull lp through first lp, beg and last lp on hook.

Cuff

Row 1 (RS): Holding 2 strands worsted yarn tog *(see Pattern Notes)* and with size J hook, ch 27, dc in 3rd ch from *hook (first 2 chs count as first dc)*, dc in each rem ch across to last st, **dc color change** *(see Stitch Guide)* to **1 strand chunky yarn** *(see Pattern Notes)* in last st, turn. Fasten off worsted yarn. *(26 dc)*

Row 2 (WS): Ch 2 *(see Pattern Notes)*, dc in each dc across to beg 2 sk chs, dc color change to worsted yarn in 2nd ch of beg 2 sk chs, fasten off chunky yarn, turn. *(26 dc)*

Row 3: Ch 1, sc in each of first 2 dc, *cl *(see Special Stitches)* in next st, sc in each of next 2 dc, rep from * across, working a **sc color change** *(see Stitch Guide)* to chunky yarn in last st, fasten off worsted yarn, turn.

Row 4: Ch 2, dc in each sc and in each cl across working dc color change to worsted yarn in last st, fasten off chunky yarn, turn.

Row 5: Ch 2, dc in each dc across, working dc color change to chunky yarn in last st, fasten off worsted yarn, turn.

Row 6: Ch 2, dc in each dc across, do not change yarns, turn.

Row 7: Ch 2, change to size F crochet hook, ***bead sc** *(see Special Stitches)* in next dc, dc in next dc, rep from * across, ending with dc color change to worsted yarn and size J hook in last st, fasten off chunky yarn, turn.

Row 8: Ch 2, dc in each sc and each dc across, ending with dc color change to chunky yarn in last st, fasten off worsted yarn, turn.

Row 9: Ch 2, change to size F crochet hook, *bead sc in next dc, dc in next dc, rep from * across, ending with a dc in the last 2 sts, do not change yarns, turn.

Row 10: Change to J crochet hook, ch 2, dc in each sc and each dc across, ending with dc color change to worsted yarn in last st, fasten off chunky yarn, turn.

Row 11: Ch 2, dc in each dc across, ending with dc color change to chunky yarn in last st, fasten off worsted yarn, turn.

Row 12: Ch 2, dc in each dc across, ending with dc color change to worsted yarn in last st, fasten off chunky yarn, turn.

Row 13: Ch 1, sc in first 2 dc, *cl in next st, sc in next 2 dc, rep from * across, working sc color change to chunky yarn in last st, fasten off worsted yarn, turn.

Row 14: Ch 2, dc in each sc and in each cl across, ending with dc color change to worsted yarn in last st, fasten off chunky yarn, turn.

Row 15: Ch 2, dc in each dc across, leaving a long tail, fasten off. *(26 dc)*

Finishing

Fold cuff in half RS tog, thread a tapestry needle with long tail at end of row 15, working through sts on both sides, sew tog. Turn RS out.

Cut 6 pieces of ribbon each 6 inches long, fold in half and sew ends of 3 each evenly across top and bottom of cuff. ●

Bowl of Cherries Muff

Design by Annie's

Skill Level

 ■■□□ EASY

Finished Measurements

11 inches long x 13 inches in circumference

Materials

- Medium (worsted) weight acrylic yarn:
  5 oz/260 yds/140g blue
- Size J/10/6mm crochet hook or size needed to obtain gauge
- 10½ inches of ⅝-inch-wide ribbon of choice
- Tapestry needle
- Materials listed for each Embellishment used

Gauge

2 clusters in pattern = 3½ inches

Pattern Notes

Chain-3 at beginning of each row counts as first double crochet unless otherwise stated.

Hold 2 strands together throughout pattern.

Embellish as desired or as shown using listed Embellishments.

Special Stitch

Cluster (cl): Holding back last lp of each st on hook, 5 tr in next st, yo, pull through all lps on hook.

Embellishments Used

1 Floral Delight *(on page 25)*

1 Cherries *(on page 26)*

1 decorative button

Muff

Row 1: Holding 2 strands tog *(see Pattern Notes)*, ch 32, sc in 2nd ch from hook and in each rem ch across, turn. *(31 sc)*

Row 2 (RS): Ch 3 *(see Pattern Notes)*, 2 dc in first sc; *sk next 2 sc, sc in next sc, sk next 2 sc, 5 dc in next sc; rep from * across to last sc; 3 dc in last sc; turn.

Row 3: Ch 1, sc in first dc; *ch 3, **cl** *(see Special Stitch)* in next sc; ch 3, sk next 2 dc, sc in next dc; rep from

* across to last 2 dc; ch 3, sk next 2 dc, sc in 3rd ch of turning ch-3; turn.

Row 4: Ch 3, 2 dc in first sc; *sc in next cl, 5 dc in next sc; rep from * across to last sc; 3 dc in last sc; turn.

Rep rows 3 and 4 for pattern until piece is 13 inches long, fasten off leaving a long tail.

Finishing

Fold design in half from top to bottom, RS tog, thread tapestry needle with the long tail at end of the piece, working through sts on both sides, sl st evenly in sts down the piece.

Cut ribbon into 3 pieces each 3½ inches long. Fold 1 length in half, pull fold through st, pull ends through fold, pull to tighten.

Evenly sp ribbons as shown in photo.

Embellish as desired or as shown in photo. ●

Sunburst

Design by Darla Sims

Skill Level

 ■■□□ EASY

Finished Measurement

6 inches in diameter

Materials

- Medium (worsted) weight acrylic yarn:
  Small amount each of 3 colors of choice
- Size H/8/5mm crochet hook
- Tapestry needle
- Stitch marker

4 MEDIUM

Gauge

Gauge is not important for this project.

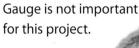

Pattern Note

Weave in ends as work progresses.

Sunburst

Rnd 1: With first color, ch 2, 8 sc in 2nd ch from hook, do not join, use marker to mark rnds. *(8 sc)*

Rnd 2: 2 sc in each sc around. *(16 sc)*

Rnd 3: [Sc in next sc, 2 sc in next sc] 8 times. *(24 sc)*

Rnd 4: [Sc in each of next 2 sc, 2 sc in next sc] 8 times. *(32 sc)*

Rnd 5: [Sc in each of next 3 sc, 2 sc in next sc] 8 times, sl st in next sc, fasten off. *(40 sc)*

Inner Petals

Rnd 1: Join 2nd color with sl st in any st, [ch 5, sc in 2nd ch from hook, hdc in next ch, dc in next ch, tr in next ch, sk next 3 sc, sl st in next sc] 10 times, fasten off. *(10 petals)*

Outer Petals

Rnd 1: Working behind petals, join 3rd color with sl st in any 2nd sc of 3 sk sc, [ch 7, sc in 2nd ch from hook, hdc in next ch, dc in each of next 2 chs, tr in each of next 2 chs, sl st in center sc of 3 sk sc of previous rnd] 10 times, fasten off. *(10 petals)* ●

Hearts

Design by Lori Zeller

Skill Level

 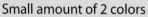 EASY

Finished Measurements

Large Heart: 4¼ inches across

Small Heart: 3½ inches across

Materials

- Medium (worsted) weight acrylic yarn:
  Small amount of 2 colors
- Size H/8/5mm crochet hook

4 MEDIUM

Gauge

Gauge is not important for this project.

Pattern Notes

May use specialty yarn for a unique look if desired.

Weave in ends as work progresses.

Join with slip stitch as indicated unless otherwise stated.

Hearts

Large Heart

Rnd 1 (RS): With color of choice, ch 3, 15 dc in 3rd ch from hook, **join** (see Pattern Notes) in top of first dc. (15 dc)

Rnd 2: Ch 1, sc in same st as joining, [hdc, dc] in next st, 3 tr in next st, [2 tr, dc] in next st, 2 dc in next st, dc in each of next 2 sts, [2 dc, ch 1, 2 dc] in next st (center bottom of heart), dc in each of next 2 sts, 2 dc in next st, [dc, 2 tr] in next st, 3 tr in next st, [dc, hdc] in next st, sc in next st, join in beg sc. (30 sts, 1 ch-1 sp)

Rnd 3: Ch 1, sc in same st as joining, [hdc, dc] in next st, 2 dc in each of next 5 sts, dc in each of next 8 sts, [2 dc, ch 1, 2 dc] in next ch-1 sp, dc in each of next 8 sts, 2 dc in each of next 5 sts, [dc, hdc] in next st, sc in next st, join in beg sc, fasten off. (46 sts, 1 ch-1 sp)

Edging

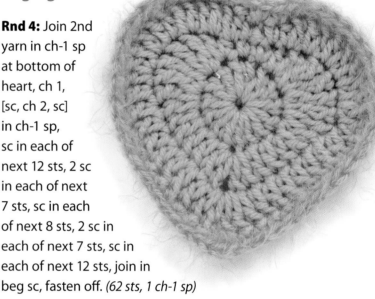

Rnd 4: Join 2nd yarn in ch-1 sp at bottom of heart, ch 1, [sc, ch 2, sc] in ch-1 sp, sc in each of next 12 sts, 2 sc in each of next 7 sts, sc in each of next 8 sts, 2 sc in each of next 7 sts, sc in each of next 12 sts, join in beg sc, fasten off. (62 sts, 1 ch-1 sp)

Small Heart

Rnd 1 (RS): With color of choice, ch 3, 15 dc in 3rd ch from hook, **join** (see Pattern Notes) in top of first dc. (15 dc)

Rnd 2: Ch 1, sc in same st as joining, [hdc, dc] in next st, 3 tr in next st, [2 tr, dc] in next st, 2 dc in next st, dc in each of next 2 sts, [2 dc, ch 1, 2 dc] in next st (center bottom of heart), dc in each of next 2 sts, 2 dc in next st, [dc, 2 tr] in next st, 3 tr in next st, [dc, hdc] in next st, sc in next st, join in beg sc. Fasten off. (30 sts, 1 ch-1 sp)

Edging

Rnd 3: Join in ch-1 sp at bottom of heart, sc in each st around, join in beg sc. Fasten off. ●

Curlicue

Design by Annie's

Skill Level

 EASY

Finished Measurement

3½ inches long

Materials

- Medium (worsted) weight acrylic yarn:
  Small amount
- Size H/8/5mm crochet hook

Gauge

Gauge is not important for this project.

Curlicue

Ch 12, 2 dc in 3rd ch from hook, 3 dc in each ch across to last ch, 2 hdc in last ch. Fasten off. ●

Zinnia

Design by Patricia Hall

Skill Level

 EASY

Finished Measurement

3½ inches in diameter

Materials

- Medium (worsted) weight acrylic yarn:
  Small amount color of choice
- Size F/5/3.75mm crochet hook
- 1 10mm bead (optional)
- Stitch marker

Gauge

Gauge is not important for this project.

Pattern Notes

Do not join rounds unless otherwise stated. Mark first stitch of each round.

Join with slip stitch as indicated unless otherwise stated.

Zinnia

Base

Rnd 1: Ch 2, 5 sc in 2nd ch from hook, **do not join, place marker** (see Pattern Notes). (5 sc)

Rnd 2: 2 sc in each st around. (10 sc)

Rnd 3: Working in **back lps** (see Stitch Guide), 2 sc in each st around. (20 sc)

Rnd 4: Working in back lps, sc in each st around.

Rnd 5: Working in back lps, [sc in next st, 2 sc in next st] around. (30 sc)

Rnd 6: Working in back lps, sc in each st around, **join** (see Pattern Notes) in beg sc. Fasten off.

Petals

Working in **front lps** (see Stitch Guide), sc in any st of rnd 2, (ch 2, dc, ch 2, sc) in same st, (sc, ch 2, dc, ch 2, sc) in each st around, continue to work in each st around rnds 3–5. At end of last rnd, join with in beg sc of first petal on rnd 5. Fasten off.

Finishing

Tack bead to center of Zinnia if desired. ●

Pompoms

Skill Level
■■□□ EASY

Materials

- Medium (worsted) weight acrylic yarn:
    Small amount color of choice
- Pompom maker

4 MEDIUM

Pompom

Work according to manufacturer instructions on pompom maker. ●

Tassel

Design by Annie's

Skill Level
■■□□ EASY

Finished Measurement

4½ inches long

Materials

- Medium (worsted) weight acrylic yarn:
    Small amount color of choice

4 MEDIUM

Tassel

Cut 22 strands each 8 inches long. Lay 2 strands to the side.

Tie 1 strand that you laid aside around center of rem 20 (see illustration A). Leaving ends free for attachment.

Wrap rem strand around all strands 1 inch below fold (see illustration B). Secure end.

Use free ends to attach to corners or as shown in photo. ●

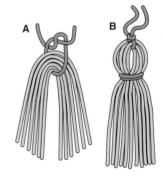

Tassel

Fish

Design by Michele Wilcox

Skill Level

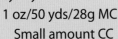 EASY

Finished Measurement

5½ inches long

Materials

- Medium (worsted) weight acrylic yarn:
  1 oz/50 yds/28g MC
  Small amount CC
- Size 10 crochet cotton:
  10 yds black
- Size G/6/4mm crochet hook or size needed to obtain gauge
- 1 blue 15mm Enami Eye
- Tapestry needle

4 MEDIUM

Gauge

4 sc = 1 inch; 4 sc rows = 1 inch

Fish

Row 1: With MC, ch 2, 3 sc in 2nd ch from hook, turn. *(3 sc)*

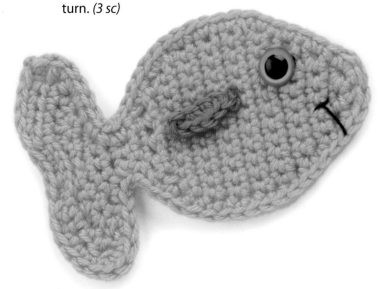

Row 2: Ch 1, sc in first st, 2 sc in next st, sc in last st, turn. *(4 sc)*

Rows 3 & 4: Ch 1, 2 sc in first st, sc in each st across with 2 sc in last st, turn. *(8 sc)*

Row 5: Ch 1, sc in each st across, turn.

Rows 6 & 7: Rep row 3. *(12 sc)*

Rows 8–14: Ch 1, sc in each st across, turn.

Rows 15 & 16: Ch 1, **sc dec** *(see Stitch Guide)* in first 2 sts, sc in each st across to last 2 sts, sc dec in last 2 sts, turn. *(8 sc)*

Row 17: Ch 1, [sc dec in next 2 sts] across, turn. *(4 sc)*

Row 18: Ch 1, sc in each st across, turn.

Row 19: Ch 1, sc dec in first 2 sts, sc dec in last 2 sts, turn. *(2 sc)*

Row 20: Ch 1, sc in each st across, turn.

Rows 21 & 22: Ch 1, 2 sc in each st across, turn. *(8 sc)*

Row 23: Ch 1, 2 sc in first st, sc in each of next 2 sts, sl st in each of next 2 sts, sc in each of next 2 sts, 2 sc in last st, turn. *(10 sts)*

Row 24: Ch 2 *(counts as first hdc)*, hdc in same st, 2 hdc in next st, hdc in next st, ch 1, sl st in each of next 4 sts, ch 1, hdc in next st, 2 hdc in each of last 2 sts, turn. *(14 sts, 2 ch sps)*

Row 25: Ch 2, hdc in each of next 4 sts, ch 1, sl st in next ch sp, sl st in each of next 4 sts, sl st in next ch-1 sp, ch 1, hdc in each of last 5 sts, turn. *(16 sts, 2 ch sps)*

Rnd 26: Now working in rnds around outer edge, ch 1, sc in each of first 5 sts, sk next ch sp, sc in each of next 2 sl sts, sc dec in next 2 sl sts, sc in each of next 2 sl sts, sk next ch sp, sc in each of next 4 sts, 3 sc in last st, evenly sp 26 sc across ends of rows, 3 sc in starting ch on opposite side of row 1, evenly sp 26 sc across ends of rows, 2 sc in same st as first sc, join in beg sc. Fasten off.

Finishing

Attach eye centered between rows 4 and 5.

With black crochet cotton, using **straight stitch** *(see illustration)*, embroider mouth lines as shown in photo.

Straight Stitch

Side Fin

With CC, ch 6, 2 sc 3rd ch from hook, hdc in next ch, sc in next ch, sl st in last ch. Fasten off.

Sew on side of Body as shown in photo. ●

Frilly Flower

Design by Darla Sims

Skill Level

 EASY

Finished Measurement

3 inches in diameter

Materials

- Medium (worsted) weight acrylic yarn:
  Small amount of 2 colors of choice
- Size H/8/5mm crochet hook

4 MEDIUM

Gauge

Gauge is not important for this project.

Pattern Notes

Weave in ends as work progresses.

Join with slip stitch as indicated unless otherwise stated.

To make a flower with more petals as seen in Cool Water Mat on page 4, follow instructions in brackets.

Flower

Rnd 1: With first color, ch 2, (10 [13] sc) sc in 2nd ch from hook, **join** *(see Pattern Notes)* in beg sc, draw up a lp of next color, fasten off first color. *(10 [13] sc)*

Rnd 2: Sl st in top of first sc, [(ch 10, sl st) in same sc, sl st in next sc] around, fasten off. *(10 [13] petals)* ●

Beaded Strings

Design by Annie's

Skill Level

 EASY

Finished Measurement

Varies

Materials
- Medium (worsted) weight acrylic yarn:
  Small amount color of choice
- Size G/6/4mm crochet hook
- 12 beads or amount needed
- 2 decorative buttons *(optional)*

4 MEDIUM

Beaded String

Decorative Button

Cut 7-inch length of yarn. Thread through 6 beads, through both holes on decorative button and back up through beads. Using yarn ends, attach to item.

This can be used as tails on other embellishments.

Knotted Ends

Place 6 beads on length of yarn, tie knot at end to hold beads in place. Attach yarn to item, place 6 more beads on yarn and tie knot in rem end to hold beads in place.

Crochet String

Leaving long end, ch 6, [drop lp from hook, insert hook in hole of bead (you may have to use a smaller hook for this), pull lp through hole, ch 3] as many times as desired to attach as many beads as you would like, ch 3 once more so that you end with 6 chs and fasten off. Tie 1 decorative button to each end. ●

Star

Design by Melissa Bennett

Skill Level

 EASY

Finished Measurement

3 inches across

Materials
- Medium (worsted) weight acrylic yarn:
  Small amount color of choice
- Size H/8/5mm crochet hook or size needed to obtain gauge
- 6mm pony beads if desired: 5
- Tapestry needle
- Sewing needle and thread

4 MEDIUM

Gauge

4 sc = 1 inch

Pattern Notes

Weave in ends as work progresses.

Join with slip stitch as indicated unless otherwise stated.

Star

Rnd 1: Ch 3, 14 dc in 3rd ch from hook, **join** *(see Pattern Notes)* in 3rd ch of ch-3. *(15 dc)*

Rnd 2: Sl st in next dc, [ch 4, sc in 2nd ch from hook, hdc in next ch, dc in next ch, sk next dc on rnd 1, sl st in each of next 2 dc] 5 times. Fasten off. *(5 star points)*

Sew pony bead to each point of Star. ●

Covered Rings

Design by Annie's

Skill Level

■■□□ EASY

Finished Measurement

1 inch

Materials

- Medium (worsted) weight acrylic yarn:
  Small amount color of choice
- Size F/5/3.75mm crochet hook
- 1-inch white bone ring
- Tapestry needle

Gauge

Gauge is not important for this project

Covered Ring

Working around ring, join with sl st, **sc around ring** *(see illustration)* until ring is covered. Fasten off.

Covered Ring With Tails

Leaving long tail, work Covered Ring until covered, leaving ¼-inch sp uncovered. Leaving long tail, fasten off.

Cut several long strands of yarn and using **lark's head knot** *(see illustration)*, attach long strands to ring in uncovered sp.

You may leave yarn as is or you can braid it or add beads to tails. ●

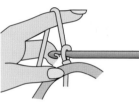
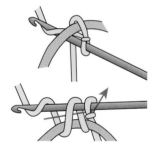

Single Crochet Around Ring

Lark's Head Knot

Mouse

Design by Michele Wilcox

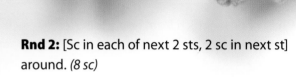

Skill Level

 EASY

Finished Measurement

3½ inches long, not including tail

Materials

- Medium (worsted) weight acrylic yarn:
    1 oz/50 yds/28g color of choice

  4 MEDIUM

- Size 10 crochet cotton:
    25 yds black

  0 LACE

- Size G/6/4mm crochet hook or size needed to obtain gauge
- 2 black 5mm beads
- Polyester fiberfill
- Tapestry needle
- Stitch marker

Gauge

4 sc = 1 inch; 4 sc rows = 1 inch

Pattern Notes

Do not join rounds unless otherwise stated. Mark first stitch of each round.

Join with slip stitch as indicated unless otherwise stated.

Mouse

Body

Rnd 1: Beg at tip of nose, with worsted yarn, ch 2, 6 sc in 2nd ch from hook, **do not join** (see Pattern Notes). (6 sc)

Rnd 2: [Sc in each of next 2 sts, 2 sc in next st] around. (8 sc)

Rnd 3: [Sc in each of next 3 sts, 2 sc in next st] around. (10 sc)

Rnd 4: [Sc in each of next 4 sts, 2 sc in next st] around. (12 sc)

Rnds 5 & 6: Sc in each st around.

Rnd 7: 2 sc in each of first 6 sts, sc in each of last 6 sts. (18 sc)

Attach 5mm beads for eyes 3 sts apart between rnds 2 and 3, centered under the 6 inc of rnd 7.

Rnds 8–14: Sc in each st around. At end last row, stuff; continue stuffing as you work.

Rnd 15: [Sc in next st, **sc dec** (see Stitch Guide) in next 2 sts] around. (12 sc)

Rnd 16: [Sc dec in next 2 sts] around, **join** (see Pattern Notes) in beg sc. Leaving long strand for weaving, fasten off.

Weave strand through sts of last rnd, pull to gather; secure.

Ear

Make 2.

With worsted yarn, ch 2, 4 sc in 2nd ch from hook, join in beg sc. Leaving long strand for sewing, fasten off.